FEATHERED FRIENDS

CARDINALS

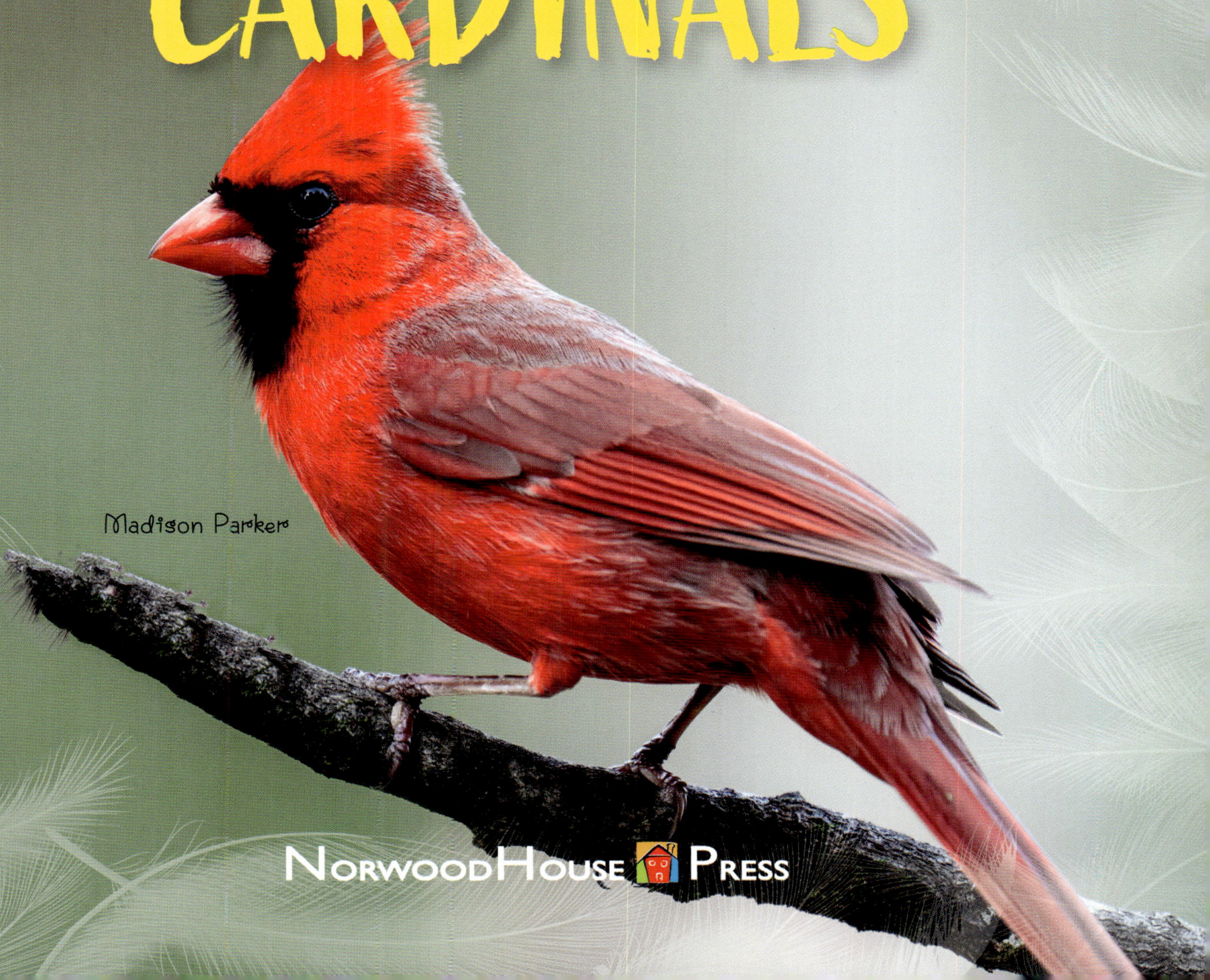

Madison Parker

NORWOOD HOUSE PRESS

Library of Congress Cataloging-in-Publication Data:

Names: Parker, Madison.
Title: Cardinals / Madison Parker.
Description: Buffalo, NY : Norwood House Press, 2025. | Series: Feathered friends | Includes glossary and index.
Identifiers: ISBN 9781684502806 (pbk.) | ISBN 9781684502813 (library bound) | ISBN 9781684502820 (ebook)
Subjects: LCSH: Cardinals (Birds)--Juvenile literature.
Classification: LCC QL696.P2438 P375 2025 | DDC 598.8'83--dc23

Published in 2025 by
Norwood House Press
2544 Clinton Street
Buffalo, NY 14224

Designer: Ocean Books
Editor: Kim Thompson

Photo credits: Cover, p. 1 SEAHABO/Shutterstock.com; p. 5 Rob Palmer Photography/Shutterstock.com; p. 6 Jepp Eaverly/Shutterstock.com; pp. 7, 12, 19 Bonnie Taylor Barry/Shutterstock.com; p. 9 Cathleen Wake Gorbatenko/Shutterstock.com; p. 11 Tara Melinda/Shutterstock.com; p. 13 Don Pope/Shutterstock.com; p. 15 WoodsyPhotos/Shutterstock.com; p. 16 Tom Franks/Shutterstock.com; p. 18 Thomas Torget/Shutterstock.com; p. 21 Danita Delimont/Shutterstock.com

Printed in the United States of America

CPSIA compliance information: Batch #CW25NHP: For further information contact Norwood House Press at 1-800-237-9932.

TABLE OF CONTENTS

What Do Cardinals Look Like?

Cardinals are our feathered friends. These birds have **crests** on their heads. Their **beaks** are orange. They have long, pointy tails.

Males are very red. Females are brown with red **highlights**.

Both males and females have a black **mask**. The mask is darker on males.

Where Do Cardinals Live?

Cardinals live in the eastern part of the United States. They also live in Mexico and Central America.

They build nests in bushes or small trees. Their nests are made from twigs and lined with grass.

How Do Cardinals Grow Up?

Cardinal eggs are pale blue or green with brown spots. It takes 12 to 13 days for baby cardinals to **hatch**. The babies grow quickly, and they are ready to fly in just three weeks.

What Do Cardinals Eat?

Cardinals like to eat seeds and fruits. They use their strong beaks to crack open seeds easily.

They also eat insects, especially during the summer. Protein from bugs gives them extra energy.

Cardinals feed insects to their babies. They carry food to the nest in their beaks. This helps their young grow strong and healthy.

What Sounds Do Cardinals Make?

A cardinal's call has a lovely sound. It sounds like "cheer, cheer, cheer."

Cardinals sing long songs with clear notes. Their songs are **complex** and beautiful.

Cardinals chirp and click to talk to each other. This helps them stay close to their families.

They sing a lot in spring and summer. Listen, and you will hear their songs often during these seasons.

What Funny Things Can Cardinals Do?

Cardinals toss seeds into the air before eating. They chase each other for fun. Sometimes, they **peck** at their **reflections** in windows.

GLOSSARY

beaks (beeks): horny, pointed jaws on birds; bird bills

complex (kuhm-PLEKS): complicated; having a large number of parts

crests (krests): tufts of feathers on the top of a bird's head

hatch (hach): to break out of an egg to be born

highlights (HYE-lites): areas that have a lighter or brighter color

mask (mask): an area of darker color across the eyes

peck (pek): to strike something or pick something up with the beak

reflections (ri-FLEK-shuhnz): images of yourself shown in glass or a mirror

THINKING QUESTIONS

1. What does a cardinal look like?
2. What is special about the sounds a cardinal makes?
3. How does a cardinal show it is smart?
4. What do cardinals eat?
5. Why do you think a cardinal is a feathered friend?

INDEX

ABOUT THE AUTHOR

Madison Parker spent her childhood in the city of Chicago, Illinois. A farm girl at heart, today she lives in Wisconsin with her husband and four children on a small farm with cows, goats, chickens, and two miniature horses named Harley and David. Her favorite dessert is vanilla frozen custard with rainbow sprinkles, even in the winter.